Best Kids' School Jokes EVER!

D1328639

Cover Art by Brian Michael Weaver
Contributing Illustrators: David Arumi, David Coulson, Briana Dengoue,
Kelly Kennedy, Pat Lewis, Rich Powell, Kevin Rechin, Brian Michael Weaver,
Karl West, Pete Whitehead

Copyright © 2022 by Highlights for Children
All rights reserved. Copying or digitizing this book for storage,
display, or distribution in any other medium is strictly prohibited.

For information about permission to reprint selections from this book,
please contact permissions@highlights.com.

Published by Highlights Press
815 Church Street
Honesdale, Pennsylvania 18431
ISBN: 978-1-64472-333-3
Library of Congress Control Number: 2021950413

Printed in Mattoon, IL, USA
Mfg. 03/2022

First edition
Visit our website at Highlights.com.
10 9 8 7 6 5 4 3 2 1

CONTENTS

CLASSROOM CHUCKLES

What did the ghost teacher say to the class?

"Look at the board, and I will go through it again."

When are kids most likely to go to school?

When the door is open.

Why did the new boy steal a chair from the classroom?

Because the teacher told him to take a seat

Why did the dog study before class?

In case the teacher gave a pup quiz.

Knock, knock.

Who's there?

Raisin.

Raisin who?

We're raisin our hands before we speak.

Devon: Did you hear about the boy who did his math test with his feet?

Laury: No. How did he do?

Devon: His answers were toe-tally wrong.

Which state asks a lot of questions?

Why-oming

What does an orange do when it takes a test?

It concentrates.

Why did the girl borrow her dad's credit card and bring it to school?

She wanted extra credit.

Why did the dollar do so well in school?

It was paying attention.

What kind of tests do they give in witch school?

Hex-aminations

Which state has the highest grades?

Alabama, because it has four As and one B.

What is a pirate's favorite subject?

ARRRR*T*

Why should you never dot another student's *i*'s?

You should always keep your i's *on your own paper.*

What animal cheats at exams?

The cheat-ah

What did the bubble gum say when it got the wrong answer?

"I blew it."

Alli: What does *IDK* mean?

Teacher: I don't know.

Alli: You're the fifth person I've asked. Nobody knows what it means!

What do sheep like to paint in art class?

Lamb-scapes

How do you get 27 students to carve a statue?

Just have everybody chip in.

Aiko: Hooray! The teacher said we will have a test, rain or shine.

Dan: Then why are you so happy?

Aiko: It's snowing!

Teacher: Order in the classroom, please!

Wyatt: I'll have a burger and fries. Thank you!

What must you pay to go to school?

Attention

What is a music student's favorite food?

Jam

Why didn't the clown use hair oil before the big test at school?

He didn't want anything to slip his mind.

Knock, knock.

Who's there?

Omelet.

Omelet who?

Omelet smarter than you think!

Teacher: How did you do with the test questions?

Harper: Great! I just had trouble with the answers.

Which mountain is the sleepiest in school?

Mount Ever-rest

What is a cow's favorite school subject?

Moo-sic

What do you call a
musical insect?

A humbug

How are a train and an orchestra alike?

They both have conductors.

Why can't you bring a
chicken to school?

*It might use fowl
language.*

What type of cheese gets in trouble for talking
too much?

Chatter cheese

Principal: Jordan, what have
you been doing in class lately?

Jordan: Nothing!

Principal: That's exactly what
your teacher said.

Knock, knock.

Who's there?

Annie.

Annie who?

Is there Annie way we can take the
test tomorrow?

What do you call students who check out a lot of books about gardening?

Good weeders

Posie: Nurse, nurse! I was playing the harmonica in music class, and I swallowed it.

School Nurse: You're lucky you weren't playing the piano!

Mrs. Yang: Billy, how do you like trampolining in gym class?

Billy: Oh, up and down, you know.

What did the apple do in gym class?

Work on its core

Why was the clock sent to the principal's office?

Because it was tocking too much

Why is bread the least motivated in school?

It just loafs around.

What did the cheese teacher say to the cheese students at the end of the day?

"You're dis-Swiss-ed."

Why was the child's report card all wet?

Because it was under C level

Teacher: Didn't I tell you to please go stand at the end of the line?

Sojiro: I did, but there was already someone else standing there.

What is white when it's dirty but black when it's clean?

A blackboard

WHEELS ON THE BUS

Knock, knock.

Who's there?

Gecko.

Gecko who?

Gecko-ing, or you'll be late for school!

Why didn't the banana go to school?

Because it wasn't peeling well

What is a bus you can never enter?

A syllabus

Teacher: Mason, why are you crawling?

Mason: Because you told us not to walk into class late.

What school did the alphabet go to?

L-M-N-tary

Teacher: You should have been here at eight o'clock!

Macy: Why? What happened?

How does a snowman get to school?

By icicle

Knock, knock.

Who's there?

Butter.

Butter who?

Butter bring an umbrella to the bus stop—looks like rain!

What did the bus driver say to the frog?

"Hop on!"

Mario: Did you know that Abraham Lincoln had to walk miles to school every day?

Thomas: Well, he should have gotten up earlier and caught the school bus like everyone else!

Why was the broom late for school?

It over-swept.

What lives in the sea and carries a lot of people?

An octo-bus

What do you call a pirate who skips school?

Captain Hooky

Knock, knock.

Who's there?

Misty.

Misty who?

Misty bus. Can I get a ride?

What does the dog teacher ride to school?

A mutt-orcycle

Princess: Why were you late for school today?

Jeremy: I was dreaming about a football game, and it went into overtime.

Knock, knock.

Who's there?

Rice.

Rice who?

Rice and shine—it's the first day of school!

Why did the chicken stay home from school?

It had the people pox.

Mom: Time to get up, Liam. It's five to eight.

Liam: Who's winning?

What did the father buffalo say to his kid when he dropped him off at school?

"Bison."

Knock, knock.

Who's there?

Ivan.

Ivan who?

Ivan to pack my lunch in the morning.

Margie: What was that loud noise?

Alice: My backpack fell on the floor.

Margie: Why did your backpack make such a loud noise?

Alice: Because I was wearing it when it fell!

How can you tell a school bus from a grape?

Jump on one for a while. If you don't get any juice, it's a school bus.

Teacher: Why were you late for school today, Albert?

Albert: I was obeying the sign that said, "Go Slow—School Ahead."

How do bees get to school?

On a school buzz

Knock, knock.

Who's there?

Cheese.

Cheese who?

Cheese riding the bus home today.

Grandpa: Why didn't you take the bus home?

India: I tried, but it wouldn't fit in my backpack.

What did the molecule's mom say to him every morning?

"Up and atom!"

What is yellow on the outside and gray on the inside?

A school bus full of elephants

Knock, knock.

Who's there?

Wafer.

Wafer who?

Wafer the bus at the corner.

Kendra: Dave, were you late for school again?

Dave: Yes, but didn't Miss Rodriguez say that it's never too late to learn?

Why didn't the zombie go to school?

He felt rotten.

Knock, knock.

Who's there?

Ketchup.

Ketchup who?

Ketchup, or else you'll miss the school bus!

What's the hardest thing about falling out of bed on the first day of school?

The floor

Dad: What did you learn in school today?

Noah: Not enough. I've got to go back tomorrow!

Why did the bat miss the bus?

It hung around for too long.

Knock, knock.

Who's there?

Irish.

Irish who?

Irish it was still summer vacation!

SILLY SUPPLIES

How does a hog do its schoolwork?

With a pigpen

How do you get straight As?

Use a ruler.

What did the boy say when he spilled glue on his hands?

"This is a sticky situation."

What does glue have for dessert?

A paste-ry

Knock, knock.

Who's there?

Pencil.

Pencil who?

Pencil fall down if you don't wear a belt.

Which Mexican food is like a ruler?

An inch-ilada

What's yellow and writes?

A ballpoint banana

Why did the student bring scissors to school?

He wanted to cut class.

What school supply is always tired?

A knapsack

What did the pencil say to the paper?

"I dot my i's on you."

Why did Julius Caesar buy crayons?

He wanted to Mark Antony.

What is an art teacher's favorite fruit?

Crayon-berries

Why did the boy put a ruler next to his bed?

Because he wanted to see how long he slept

Annabelle: What brand of pencils do you want?

Kathy: I want brand-new pencils!

What did the pen say to the pencil?

"So, what's your point?"

What kind of pen wears a wig?

A bald-point pen

What did one calculator say to the other?

"You can count on me."

How do you put a broken ruler back together?

Use measuring tape.

Which hand is better to write with?

Neither—you should use a pen!

What kind of pencil fixes cars?

A mechanical pencil

What did the glue stick say to the eraser?

Nothing. Glue sticks can't talk!

What coin can you write with?

A penny

Where are pencils made?

Pencil-vania

Knock, knock.

Who's there?

Glue.

Glue who?

Glue you know where I can find some more paper?

What has three feet but no toes?

A yardstick

What did the paper say to the glue?

"Let's stick together."

Who is the king of the classroom?

The ruler

What did the pepperoni say when it needed to take notes?

"May I have a pizza paper and a pen?"

What tools do you need for math?

Multi-pliers

What do you get when you cross a piece of paper with a pair of scissors?

A paper cut

What do artists use when they are sleepy?

Cra-yawns

Knock, knock.

Who's there?

A broken pencil.

A broken pencil who?

Oh, never mind. It's pointless.

What did the paper say to the pen?

"Write on!"

What happened when the pigpen broke?

The pig had to use a pencil.

What did the janitor say when he jumped out of the closet?

"Supplies!"

ROLL CALL

Knock, knock.

Who's there?

Abby.

Abby who?

Abby stung me on my nose at recess.

Knock, knock.

Who's there?

Alex.

Alex who?

Alex the questions around here.

Knock, knock.

Who's there?

Ahmed.

Ahmed who?

Ahmed a big mistake on the test today!

Knock, knock.

Who's there?

Anita.

Anita who?

Anita tissue, please.

Knock, knock.

Who's there?

Barry.

Barry who?

Barry nice to see you in class!

Knock, knock.

Who's there?

Blair.

Blair who?

Blair are you going? The bus is over here!

Knock, knock.

Who's there?

Carl.

Carl who?

A Carl get you to school faster than a bike.

Knock, knock.

Who's there?

Carrie.

Carrie who?

Carrie-ing numerals is important for math.

Knock, knock.

Who's there?

Cathy.

Cathy who?

Cathy anything with this blindfold on!

Knock, knock.

Who's there?

Diego.

Diego who?

Diego before the *B*.

Knock, knock.

Who's there?

Divya.

Divya who?

Divya hear the joke about the kid at recess?

Knock, knock.

Who's there?

Gabe.

Gabe who?

I Gabe it everything I've got, but I still can't do a handstand.

Knock, knock.

Who's there?

Harmony.

Harmony who?

Harmony times do I have to tell you to sit down?

Knock, knock.

Who's there?

Ida.

Ida who?

Ida sandwich for lunch. What'd you have?

Knock, knock.

Who's there?

Jess.

Jess who?

Jess me and my shadow.

Knock, knock.

Who's there?

Jewel.

Jewel who?

Jewel be happy when I tell you what they're serving for lunch.

Knock, knock.

Who's there?

Keith.

Keith who?

Keith going—what happened next?

Knock, knock.

Who's there?

Lena.

Lena who?

Lena little closer— I have something to tell you.

Knock, knock.

Who's there?

Marcus.

Marcus who?

Marcus both down for the school talent show!

Knock, knock.

Who's there?

Noah.

Noah who?

Noah good joke about school?

Knock, knock.

Who's there?

Norma Lee.

Norma Lee who?

Norma Lee I'd be in school right now, but we have the day off.

Knock, knock.

Who's there?

Omar.

Omar who?

Omar goodness, wrong classroom door!

Knock, knock.

Who's there?

Oswald.

Oswald who?

Oswald my bubble gum.

—Gulp!

Knock, knock.

Who's there?

Paul.

Paul who?

Paul up a chair, and I'll tell you.

Knock, knock.

Who's there?

Stacey.

Stacey who?

Stacey-ted until the bus stops.

Knock, knock.

Who's there?

Tamara.

Tamara who?

Tamara is another school day.

Knock, knock.

Who's there?

Thaddeus.

Thaddeus who?

To be or not to be. Thaddeus the question.

Knock, knock.

Who's there?

Tyrone.

Tyrone who?

Tyrone shoelaces, please.

Knock, knock.

Who's there?

Uriah.

Uriah who?

Keep Uriah on your own paper!

Knock, knock.

Who's there?

Victor.

Victor who?

Victor his pants when he bent over.

Knock, knock.

Who's there?

Wayne.

Wayne who?

Wayne is the spelling test?

Knock, knock.

Who's there?

Wei.

Wei who?

Which Wei is the cafeteria?

ENTERTAINING ENGLISH

What do elves learn in school?

The elf-abet

What speaks every language?

An echo

Teacher: Amelia, come and spell *mouse* in front of the class, please.

Amelia: M-O-U-S.

Teacher: What's on the end?

Amelia: A tail!

What kind of writing does a witch use?

Curse-ive

How do spiders learn definitions?

They use Webster's Dictionary.

What comes after *L*?

Bow

Pavani: Can you spell *eighty* in two letters?

Matthew: Sure! A-T.

Why was the dog excited to go to school?

The class was having a smelling bee.

When is a mailbox like the alphabet?

When it's full of letters

Teacher: What is the shortest month?

Gordon: May—it only has three letters.

What word do even teachers spell wrong?

Wrong

Teacher: Luke, please use the word *denial* in a sentence.

Luke: Denial is a river in Egypt.

What do baby bunnies learn in school?

The alfalfa-bet

What letter of the alphabet has lots of water?

The C

How do you spell *mousetrap*?

C-A-T

Joo-won: What letter does *yellow* start with?

Maria: *Y*?

Joo-won: Because I want to know!

> **When is a blue book not a blue book?**
>
> *When it's read*

Teacher: How many letters are in the alphabet?

Isla: 11.

Teacher: No, there are 26. How did you get 11?

Isla: T-H-E A-L-P-H-A-B-E-T.

> **What is a pronoun?**
>
> *A noun that gets paid*

What do you get when you throw books into the ocean?

A title wave

42

What five-letter word becomes shorter when you add two letters to it?

Short

What is smarter than a talking dog?

A spelling bee

What is the first thing a dog learns in school?

The arf-abet

Teacher: Nasrin, name two pronouns.

Nasrin: Who, me?

Teacher: That's correct.

What is the world's longest punctuation mark?

The hundred-yard dash

What did Natasha do when she saw the class rabbit eating the dictionary?

She took the words right out of his mouth.

What's a ten-letter word that starts with gas?

Automobile

Why does it take pirates so long to learn the alphabet?

Because they spend years at C

Teacher: Sarah, spell *vacuum*.

Sarah: V-A-C-W-M.

Teacher: There is no *W* in *vacuum*.

Sarah: I did not say *W*. I said double *U*.

What kind of tree grows poems?

A poetry

Teacher: Francisco, give me a sentence that is a question.

Francisco: Why do I always get the hard ones?

Teacher: Very good.

What is the longest word in the English language?

Smiles—*there is a mile between the first letter and the last letter!*

Teacher: Can you use the word *fascinate* in a sentence?

Ashley: Sure. I have ten buttons on my sweater, but I only fasten eight.

What is the first thing a monkey learns in school?

His Ape-B-C's

Teacher: Liza, what is your favorite state?

Liza: Mississippi.

Teacher: Spell it, please.

Liza: Oh, favorite state? I meant to say Ohio.

What happens when you leave alphabet soup on the stove?

It could spell disaster.

What does the letter *A* have in common with a flower?

They both have bees coming after them.

Teacher: Oliver, please use the word *arrest* in a sentence.

Oliver: After running up a steep hill, you need arrest.

Arturo: I got one wrong on my spelling test. Oh well, no one knows how to spell everything.

Emma: I do! E-V-E-R-Y-T-H-I-N-G.

Teacher: How do you spell *cow*?

Old MacDonald: C-O-W-E-I-E-I-O.

SIDE-SPLITTING SCIENCE

Why did the germ cross the microscope?

To get to the other slide

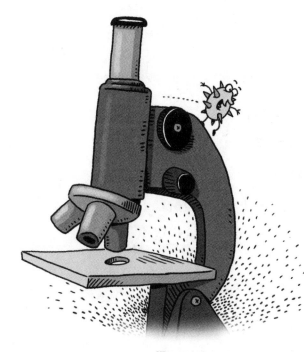

What is a wildebeest's favorite subatomic particle?

The gnu-tron

What is root beer's favorite subject?

Fizz-ics

Emmett: Did you hear about the scientist reading a book about helium?

Nora: Yes—he couldn't put it down!

Why can't you trust atoms?

They make up everything.

Atom #1: I think I just lost an electron.

Atom #2: Are you sure?

Atom #1: Yes, I'm positive.

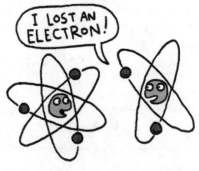

Anyone know any jokes about sodium deposits?

Na

If a moth breathes oxygen in the daytime, what does it breathe at night?

Night-rogen

Knock, knock.

Who's there?

Element.

Element who?

Element to tell you she'd be late for class today.

What did one tectonic plate say when he bumped into another?

"Sorry! My fault!"

How did the rainbow do on the science test?

It passed with flying colors.

Dr. Watson: Holmes! What kind of rock is this?

Sherlock Holmes: Sedimentary, my dear Watson.

Why is an ice cube so smart?

It has 32 degrees.

How many balls of string would it take to reach the moon?

Just one, but it would be have to be a big one.

Knock, knock.

Who's there?

Jupiter.

Jupiter who?

Jupiter fly in my soup?

Why was the moon acting so loony at school?

It was going through a phase.

How do astronomers organize a party?

They planet

Why didn't the sun go to college?

Because it already had thousands of degrees

What three letters make everything in the world move?

N, R, G

Why was there thunder and lightning in the science wing?

The teachers were brainstorming.

Teacher: Did you know grasshoppers have antennae?

Violet: Cool, do they get cable?

What do you get if you eat uranium?

Atomic-ache

What is heavy forward but not backward?

Ton

Finn: What's the matter?

Priyanka: Anything that has mass and weight.

Knock, knock.

Who's there?

Attest.

Attest who?

**Attest in science?
I'd better study!**

Jasper: Mom, I got a B on my science test!

Mom: Well, I hope it doesn't sting you.

What did the white blood cell say to the other white blood cells?

"Antibody out there?"

What can go through water and not get wet?

Sunlight

Teacher: What happens when the human body is totally submerged in water?

Guillermo: The telephone rings.

Why does lightning shock people?

Because it doesn't know how to conduct itself

What kind of dog has science as its favorite subject?

A Labrador

Where do science teachers read about volcanoes?

In magma-zines

What did the paper clip say to the magnet?

"You're so attractive!"

What kind of insects are bad at football?

Fumble-bees

Knock, knock.

Who's there?

Lava.

Lava who?

Lava good day at school.

What did one volcano say to the other?

"Stop int-erupt-ing me!"

LAUGHS FOR LUNCH

What did one tray say to the other?

"Lunch is on me today."

Why did the two 4's skip lunch?

They already 8.

Where do comedians go for lunch?

The laugh-eteria

Jackson: Let me guess what you had for lunch today. You had spaghetti and meatballs.

Mackenzie: Wow, that's amazing. Did you read my mind?

Jackson: No, your chin.

What did the macaroni say as it left the cafeteria?

"Pasta la vista!"

What kind of fish goes great on a peanut butter sandwich?

Jellyfish

Knock, knock.

Who's there?

Bacon.

Bacon who?

Bacon a cake to bring for your birthday.

What did the computer do at lunchtime?

It had a byte.

Alejandro: Would you like my apple?

Rachel: No, I don't feel like an apple.

Alejandro: That's good. You don't look like one either!

Why couldn't the egg lend his friend lunch money?

Because he was broke

What do penguins eat for lunch?

Brr-itos

How do you make a chocolate milkshake?

Give it a good scare.

Joy: I packed my own lunch today.

Kelly: What did you bring?

Joy: Uh . . . chocolate soup.

Kelly: Chocolate soup?

Joy: Well, this morning it was ice cream.

What food chats all through lunch?

A talk-o

What do math teachers do in the lunchroom?

They divide their lunches with one another.

What fruit contains barium and double sodium?

BaNaNa

Knock, knock.

Who's there?

Wanda.

Wanda who?

Wanda have another burger?

What does a camera have for lunch?

Cheese

What kind of candy is always late for class?

Chocolate

Why is spaghetti the smartest food?

It always uses its noodle.

Maile: My lunch tastes kind of funny today.

James: Then why aren't you laughing?

What do twins bring to eat for lunch?

Pears

What's bacteria?

The rear entrance to a cafeteria

Why was the cafeteria's kitchen having math problems?

Its counter was gone.

Chandra: Why is there a hot dog behind your ear?

Jack: Oops, I must have eaten my pencil for lunch.

What is a librarian's favorite lunch food?

Shush-kabob

What did the cafeteria clock do after eating its lunch?

It went back four seconds.

Teacher: Why aren't you going home for lunch?

Archie: My father told me not to leave school until I graduate.

What do ghosts eat for lunch?

Spook-etti

RIB-TICKLING RECESS

What is the trombone's favorite thing on the playground?

The slide

Knock, knock.

Who's there?

Toucan.

Toucan who?

Toucan play
this game.

What game do rabbits play
with kangaroos?

Hopscotch

Teacher: Amy, please use the word *lettuce* in
a sentence.

Amy: Please lettuce go to recess early today!

What do little bears do
when they play?

Build a cub-house

Where do explorers like to play?

A jungle gym

What do you get when you
play tug-of-war with a pig?

Pulled pork

What game do mice play at recess?

Hide-and-squeak

What do you call a boomerang that doesn't come back?

A stick

Knock, knock.

Who's there?

Freddie.

Freddie who?

Freddie or not, here I come!

Why do soccer players do so well in school?

They use their heads.

What's a baboon's favorite thing on the playground?

The monkey bars

Mel: Have you heard the joke about the jump rope?

Katya: No. Tell me.

Mel: Skip it!

Why does the schoolyard get bigger when recess starts?

It has more feet in it.

Why shouldn't you play hide-and-seek with a mountain?

It peaks!

Why did the girl cross the playground?

To get to the other slide

Knock, knock.

Who's there?

Joanna.

Joanna who?

Joanna come play with me?

What is the loudest kind of sports equipment?

A racket

What do you call a teeter-totter for donkeys?

A hee-haw *seesaw*

Teacher: What is the definition of climate?

Harry: That's what kids do when they see a tree at recess.

What do mice wear at recess?

Squeakers

What game do fish like to play?

Salmon Says

What did the *T. rex* say after he fell off the swing?

"I'm so saurus!"

Why didn't the skeleton like recess?

He had no body to play with.

Knock, knock.

Who's there?

Stew.

Stew who?

Stew early to go out for recess.

What does a piece of fruit say when it goes down a slide?

"Ki-wheee!"

What is a horse's favorite thing on the playground?

The teeter-trotter

What's the most expensive game of tag?

Price tag

Cara: I can tell you what the score will be before the kickball game starts.

Cory: No way!

Cara: Yes, I can. 0–0. It hasn't started yet!

What do you call a carousel that doesn't stop turning?

A merry-go-round-and-round-and-round . . .

Why didn't the quarter roll down the hill with the nickel?

Because it had more cents

Why did the ghost get kicked out of the kickball game?

He screamed, "Boo!"

What do pigs do when they play games at recess?

Hog the ball

Knock, knock.

Who's there?

Sincerely.

Sincerely who?

Sincerely this morning, I've been waiting for recess.

Why can't dalmatians play hide-and-seek?

They are always spotted.

What's the hardest thing about falling off the monkey bars?

The ground

SOCIAL STUDIES HEE-HEES

What do you get when you cross a U.S. president with a shark?

Jaws Washington

What was the most popular dance in 1776?

Indepen-dance

Teacher: What did they do at the Boston Tea Party?

Lily: I don't know. I wasn't invited!

Who was the biggest jokester in George Washington's army?

Laugh-ayette

What do you call an American drawing?

A Yankee doodle

How were the first Americans like ants?

They lived in colonies.

What kind of tea did the
American colonists like?

Liberty

Dad: How is your report card, Christy?

Christy: Well, Dad, I did the same thing as George Washington.

Dad: And what is that?

Christy: I went down in history.

What rock group has
four men that don't sing?

Mount Rushmore

What famous inventor loved practical jokes?

Benjamin Prank-lin

Candice: Why is the pharaoh boastful?

Kasim: I don't know. Why?

Candice: Because he sphinx he's the best.

What was purple and conquered the world?

Alexander the Grape

Who built King Arthur's round table?

Sir Cumference

Shana: Did you hear the one about the Liberty Bell?

Meira: Yeah, it cracked me up!

What did King Arthur say to his court?

"I want all of you to enroll in knight school."

Why were the early days of history called the Dark Ages?

Because there were so many knights

Where did Montezuma go to college?

Az Tech

73

What mouse was a Roman emperor?

Julius Cheese-r

Teacher: When was Rome built?

Damon: At night.

Teacher: Why do you think that?

Damon: Because my dad said, "Rome wasn't built in a day."

What explorer was the best at hide-and-seek?

Marco Polo

What's purple, long, and at least 2,300 years old?

The Grape Wall of China

Teacher: Class, please open your geography books. Who can tell me where China is?

Evelyn: I know! It's on page 20.

What do maps and fish have in common?

Both have scales

Which is smarter, longitude or latitude?

Longitude, because it has 360 degrees.

Why do paper maps never win poker tournaments?

Because they always fold

Knock, knock.

Who's there?

Abe.

Abe who?

Abe C D E F G . . .

Teacher: Lakshmi, please go to the map and locate Cuba.

Lakshmi: Here it is!

Teacher: Very good. Now, does anyone know who discovered Cuba?

Raúl: Lakshmi!

Which U.S. president liked the environment the most?

Tree-adore Roosevelt

Teacher: Do you know the 14th president of the United States?

Sandra: No, we were never introduced!

What does the president use to decorate the White House for the Fourth of July?

The Decorations of Independence

Why did the kids go to the White House and look at the trees?

They were studying the branches of government.

Why is history the fruitiest subject in school?

Because it's full of dates

Teacher: Where is the English Channel?

Reid: I don't know. My TV doesn't pick it up!

What mountain range is also a fruit?

The Apple-acian Mountains

Which state has the most streets?

Rhode Island

Which American president wore the biggest hat?

The one with the biggest head.

Knock, knock.

Who's there?

Juneau.

Juneau who?

Juneau where Alaska is?

What state is round at each end and high in the middle?

Ohio

What is a snake's favorite subject?

Hiss-*tory*

Shaun: I wish I had been born 1,000 years ago.

Cassy: Why is that?

Shaun: Just think of all the history that I wouldn't have to learn!

Why does Mississippi have the best vision out of all the states?

Because it has four i's

MATH MIRTH

Why is arithmetic hard work?

You have to carry all those numerals.

What triangles are the coldest?

Ice-osceles

What kinds of numbers live in tall grass?

Arithme-ticks

How can you make seven even?

Take away the letter S

What do you call a crushed angle?

A rectangle

Knock, knock.

Who's there?

Jamaica.

Jamaica who?

Jamaica good grade on your math test?

What is a mathematician's favorite dessert?

Pi

Why was 6 afraid of 7?

Because 7 8 9

Teacher: If I had 6 oranges in one hand and 7 in the other hand, what would I have?

Nico: Big hands!

What is a butterfly's favorite subject at school?

Moth-ematics

How did the horse learn multiplication?

Using times stables

Why was the math book sad?

Because it had too many problems

What do you call an angle that is adorable?

Acute angle

What is a math teacher's favorite sum?

Summer

Knock, knock.

Who's there?

Vaughn.

Vaughn who?

Vaughn plus Vaughn equals two.

Who invented algebra?

An X-pert

What do you call more than one *L*?

A parallel

How is 2 + 2 = 5 like your left foot?

It's not right.

Ryan: If twelve inches are a foot, what would I have if I had three feet?

Alec: Trouble finding shoes!

What did the 0 say to the 8?

"Hey, nice belt!"

What geometric figure is like a lost parrot?

A polygon

Teacher: Jenna, if I gave you two goldfish and Ijeoma gave you four goldfish, how many would you have?

Jenna: Eleven.

Teacher: Incorrect. You'd have six.

Jenna: But I already have five goldfish at home!

Why didn't the square talk to the circle?

Because there wasn't a point

What is a forum?

Two-um plus two-um

Who invented fractions?

Henry the 1/4th

Teacher: If you had 27 marbles in one pocket and 89 in the other, what would you have?

Jada: Heavy pants.

What subject do owls like to study?

Owl-gebra

Why did the student do multiplication problems on the floor?

The teacher told her not to use tables.

Teacher: Now, class, I will ask you a question, and I want you all to answer at once. What is 7 plus 8?

Class: At once!

How can you use 9 four times and make 100?

99 + 9/9

Why did the student wear glasses during math class?

Because they improve division

What do you get when you divide the circumference of a jack-o'-lantern by its diameter?

Pumpkin pi

Knock, knock.

Who's there?

Geometry.

Geometry who?

Geometry in the school play!

If two is a couple and three is a crowd, what are four and five?

Nine

What is seaweed's favorite subject?

Algae-bra

What did the plus sign say to the minus sign?

"You are so negative."

Teacher: You have 10 chocolate bars. You eat 8 of them. What do you have now?

Muhammad: A stomachache.

Why can't your nose be twelve inches long?

Because then it would be a foot

What did the nine say to the six?

"Why are you standing on your head?"

Teacher: Archer, if a man walked three miles in one hour, how many could he walk in four hours?

Archer: That depends on how tired he got in the first hour!

What part of a newspaper is like math class?

The ad section

Why did the math book go to the doctor?

It hurt its spine.

Why did the obtuse angle go to the beach after school?

Because it was over 90 degrees

What grew from the plant in the math room?

Square roots

Why did the math student divide sin by tan?

Just cos

TEACHER TEE-HEES

What do you do if a teacher rolls her eyes at you?

Pick them up and roll them back at her.

Why did the teacher wear sunglasses in school?

Because his class was so bright

Where do geology teachers like to relax?

In a rocking chair

What did the sweet potato say to the teacher?

"Here I yam!"

How is an English teacher like a judge?

They both give out sentences.

What do librarians use as bait when they go fishing?

Bookworms

Teacher: Ava, you copied Kevin's answers on the test!

Ava: How did you know?

Teacher: Because on number 11, Kevin wrote, "I don't know," and you wrote, "Me neither."

What kind of tree does a math teacher climb?

Geometry

Who is your best friend at school?

Your principal

What do you call a teacher who never says your name right?

Miss Pronounce

Skylar: How many pupils do you have?

Teacher: Two, of course!

Knock, knock.

Who's there?

Pickle.

Pickle who?

Pickle little flower for your teacher.

Why couldn't the music teacher open his classroom door?

Because his keys were on the piano

What does a fairy teacher use to correct her tests?

A magic marker

What kind of meals do math teachers eat?

Square meals

Teacher: We will have a half-day of school this morning.

Students: Hurray! Yippee!

Teacher: We will have the other half this afternoon.

Why couldn't Mozart find his teacher?

He was Haydn.

What did the lobster give to its teacher?

A crab apple

Why did the teacher write the lesson on the window?

She wanted it to be perfectly clear.

Librarian #1: Want to go to the movies on Saturday?

Librarian #2: Thanks, but my weekend is all booked.

What's a teacher's favorite nation?

Explanation

What kind of dance do teachers like best?

Attendance

What did the cat teacher say to the cat student?

"You have a purr-fect score!"

Who filled in for the ballet teacher when she was out sick?

A substi-tutu

Art teacher: What color would you paint the sun and the wind?

Imani: The sun rose and the wind blue.

How does a karate teacher greet his students?

"Hi-yah!"

Why was the karate teacher stopped at the butcher shop?

He was caught chop-lifting.

What is an English teacher's favorite breakfast?

A synonym roll

How did the teacher describe her class?

Sharp as a tack!

What do you get when you cross a vampire and a teacher?

A lot of blood tests

Why did the cyclops stop teaching?

Because he had only one pupil

Teacher: Take a seat, please.

Charlotte: Take it where?

What is a math teacher's favorite kind of candy?

Measure-mints

Why did the teacher fall in love with the janitor?

Because he swept her off her feet

Teacher: Can anyone tell me how turtles communicate?

Johnny: On their shell phones?

What do teachers drink on snowy days?

Hot chalk-olate

Why was the math teacher crying on the last day of school?

Because he didn't want to be divided from his students

Teacher: Where's your homework, Diamond?

Diamond: I don't have it. My dog ate it.

Teacher: How could your dog eat your homework?

Diamond: I fed it to him.

What is the worst thing that can happen to a geography teacher?

Getting lost

What's the difference between a train engineer and a teacher?

One minds the train and the other trains the mind.

What place in New York City do math teachers like the best?

Times Square

What do you say when comforting a grammar teacher?

"There, their, they're."

What did the art teacher say after spilling paint on a student?

"Are you all white?"

What do history teachers make when they want to meet up?

Dates

When does a teacher carry birdseed?

When she has a parrot-teacher conference

What did the music teacher send home to his students' parents?

A note

Teacher: If a tree falls in a forest and no one is there to hear it, does it make a sound?

Levi: I'm stumped.

What happened when the teacher tied all the kids' shoelaces together?

They had a class trip.

BOOKS NEVER WRITTEN

How to Learn

by Rita Book

When Does School Start?

by Winna Belrings

Where to Sit in Class

by Wayne Front

How to Get Smart

by Ed U. Cated

How to Read Novels

by Paige Turner

Tardy

by Mark M. Late

Aches and Pains

by Colin Doctor

How to Not Succeed in School

by Skip Class

Shapes

by Paul E. Gone

Who Was George Washington?

by Perez E. Dent

Signing the Declaration of Independence

by Phil A. Delphi

Before the Cocoon

by Kat R. Pillar

Checking Your Homework

by R. U. Wright

Smart People

by Gene E. Us

I Made a Mistake

by Anita Eraser

Guide to Dinosaurs

by Tara Dactyl

The Wonders of Woodwinds

by Clare E. Net

The Numbers Game

by Cal Q. Later

Backpack Uses

by Carrie Books

Two Kinds of Numbers

by Evan N. Odd

How to Draw

by Mark Er

Egyptian Structures

by P. Ramid

The Place of Disasters

by Mila Boratory

Reading My Textbook

by Lotta Letters

How to Sing

by Mel O. Dee

Gym Class Activities

by Raina Mile

Taking a Test

by B. A. Wiseman

The History of Tag

by U. R. It

The Colors of the Rainbow

by Roy G. Biv

How to Stop Procrastinating

by Mae B. Later

Floating Furniture

by Aunty Gravity

Summer School

by Nova Kayshon

After School

by Dee Tension

AFTER-SCHOOL ANTICS

Where did the whale play his violin?

In the orca-stra

Why did the ice-cream cone become editor of the school newspaper?

To get the latest scoop

What has 40 feet and sings?

The school choir

Knock, knock.

Who's there?

Pudding.

Pudding who?

Pudding on my costume for the school play!

What can't a coach ever say to a team of zombies?

"Look alive!"

What do you get when you cross a librarian with a golf coach?

A book club

Why did the sheep say *moo*?

It was in a foreign language club.

Director: Before we start auditions for the play, tell me—who has stage experience?

Sasha: My leg was in a cast once.

If two fish try out for the school choir, which one will be chosen?

The one with better scales

Why did the football coach send in his second string?

To tie up the game

What animal comes to every baseball game?

A bat

Why did the chicken cross the book?

To get to the author side

Knock, knock.

Who's there?

Teachers.

Teachers who?

Teachers for the soccer team!

What did one snail say to the other at the school dance?

"I'm really good at slow dancing."

Why was the voice teacher so good at baseball?

She had perfect pitch.

What is the world's tallest building?

The library, because it has the most stories.

Where does a donkey go on a field trip?

A mule-seum

Erin: What is the quietest sport?

DeShawn: Bowling, of course. You can hear a pin drop!

Where do vegetables go on field trips?

The zoo-chini

Why didn't the raisin go to the school dance?

It didn't have a date.

Knock, knock.

Who's there?

Tennis.

Tennis who?

Tennis five plus five

What kind of music do runners listen to?

Cross-country music

Why does the ice melt after the hockey game is over?

All the fans are gone.

Where do soccer players sit to watch the school play?

The ball-cony

What kind of plant is good at gymnastics?

Tumbleweed

Why did the teacher go to the beach after school?

To test the water

Knock, knock.

Who's there?

Abandon.

Abandon who?

Abandon the street is marching this way.

What is a cheerleader's favorite soda?

Root beer

Knock, knock.

Who's there?

Arthur.

Arthur who?

Arthur any after-school clubs I can join?

Why did the square go to the school gym?

To stay in shape

What kind of cats join the bowling team?

Alley cats

What do you get if you cross a football player and a dinosaur?

A quarterback no one can tackle

Why didn't the tree join the checkers club?

It was a chess-nut.

What kind of dance class does a tortilla chip take?

Salsa

Knock, knock.

Who's there?

Dewey.

Dewey who?

Dewey want to go on another field trip?

Where do mermaids find after-school jobs?

In the kelp-wanted section

Sam: Our school played Beethoven last night.

Ty: Who won?

Knock, knock.

Who's there?

Benjamin.

Benjamin who?

Benjamin with the marching band all day.

Where do cats go on field trips?

Mew-seums

Why did the pig want to be in the school play?

He was a big ham.

Why did the tiny ghost join the volleyball team?

They needed a little team spirit.

What animal flies around schools at night?

The alpha-bat

Knock, knock.

Who's there?

Grape.

Grape who?

Grape game you played tonight!

HOMEWORK HA-HAS

Knock, knock.

Who's there?

Vivaldi.

Vivaldi who?

Vivaldi homework I have, I'll be up all night.

What do elves do after school?

Gnome-work

Teacher: Elijah, your essay titled "My Dog" is similar to your brother's. Did you copy his?

Elijah: No, it is the same dog.

Why did the girl eat her homework?

Because she didn't have a dog

Evangeline: I got 100 in school today.

Dad: That's great! In what subject?

Evangeline: I got 50 in spelling and 50 in math.

Why did the fuzz ball need the computer for its homework?

It had to use the lint-ernet.

Teacher: For homework tonight, I want you to write an essay on your favorite president.

Logan: I'd rather write on paper.

What did the teacher do with the cheese's homework?

He grated it.

What color are books you've finished?

Red

Tate: My teacher says that I have to write more clearly.

Mom: That's a good idea.

Tate: No, it isn't. Then she'll know I can't spell.

Why did the phone always do its homework on time?

Because it was a smartphone

What kind of gum do you chew when doing your science homework?

Ex-spearmint gum

Patrick: Dad, Mr. Crawford gave me an F for this drawing.

Dad: He did? That's a great drawing! Why would he give you an F?

Patrick: Because I drew it in French class.

Why did the boy eat his homework?

The teacher told him it was a piece of cake.

Knock, knock.

Who's there?

Needle.

Needle who?

Needle little help with your homework?

Mom: Why are you having trouble in history class?

Radha: Because the teacher keeps asking about things that happened before I was born!

Why couldn't Orange understand his homework?

Because Red and Yellow were mixing him up

What do you call a book that only has pages with even numbers?

Odd

Bryant: Where does Friday come before Thursday?

Grandpa: I don't know. Where?

Bryant: In the dictionary!

Teacher: Why didn't you finish your homework?

Monster: I was full.

Knock, knock.

Who's there?

Canoe.

Canoe who?

Canoe come help me with my homework?

What do you call a boy with a dictionary in his pocket?

Smarty-pants

Teacher: Where is your homework?

Jingwen: A ghost ate it.

Teacher: I can see right through that excuse!

Why did the kid study on the airplane?

He wanted a higher education.

Dad: What did you learn in school today?

Dalia: My teacher taught us writing.

Dad: What did you write?

Dalia: I don't know. She hasn't taught us reading yet.

Mark: Do you like homework?

Marietta: I like nothing better.

Why did the ballerina have trouble finishing her lab report?

It was tutu hard.

SCHOOL-ARIOUS!

Why was the dog so good in school?

He was the teacher's pet.

Maisie: My dog's the smartest in town. She can say her own name in perfect English.

Nika: What's her name?

Maisie: Ruff.

What do vampires wear on the first day of school?

Their bat-to-school clothes

What does an alien do when it is bored in school?

It spaces out.

In what school do you learn how to greet people?

Hi school

At which school do you have to drop out
to graduate?

Parachute school

Where do fish learn to swim?

In schools

Why did the dad have to go to school?

To take his pop quiz

Shivansh: My mom says
that I get to choose my
school clothes this year.

Stefon: Oh, really?
My dog's the one that
chews mine!

Where do cats go to school?

Kitty-garten

Where do squirrels go to
school before kindergarten?

Tree school

What did the cheese say when he got his
school picture taken?

"People!"

Knock, knock.

Who's there?

Census.

Census who?

Census Saturday, we don't have to go to school.

What is a robot's favorite part of school?

Assembly

School Nurse: Have your eyes ever been checked?

Ahuva: No, they've always been blue.

What is the study of back-to-school shopping called?

Buy-ology

What kind of school do
air and water go to?

Elementary school

Zane: I didn't know our school was haunted.

Troye: Neither did I. How did you find out?

Zane: Everybody's been talking about our
school spirit!

Why does the sun seem
so bright?

Because it shines in class

Where do you learn how to make ice cream?

At sundae school

Why did the pickle go to
the nurse's office?

He felt dill.

School Nurse: Have you ever had trouble with appendicitis?

Dory: Only when I tried to spell it.

What happened to the chicken who kept misbehaving at school?

She was egg-spelled.

Why couldn't the invisible boy pass summer school?

Because the teacher always marked him absent

When do flowers go to school?

In kinder-garden

Why did the light bulb go to school?

He wanted to get brighter.

Principal: Chigozie, I hear that you missed the first day of school.

Chigozie: Yes, but I didn't miss it very much.

What do you call a duck that does well in school?

A wise-quacker

Where do owls go to school?

Owl-mentary school

School nurse: Your poison ivy will be all gone by tomorrow.

Lance: Please don't make rash promises!

Why did the boy bring a ladder to school?

He wanted to go to high school.

What will the school for race cars do after the summer?

Re-zoom

What do mama spices say to their kids on graduation day?

"Where did the thyme go?"

Knock, knock.

Who's there?

Atlas.

Atlas who?

Atlas, it's the weekend!